## About the book

This book is a collection of 40 lyrics or poems. Mostly are love poems. The author is a member of a Composer's group called Songwriter's hub (established February 26, 2018) which is headed by Sir Arnel Laquindanum. This is the inspiration shared by the author and made shareable to you. Please feel free to choose and make music to any or all of the lyrics. This won't take too much of your time. Let us share love. Giving all that we are to make a composer(s). This is the heart of a composer.

This book is dedicated to the members of Songwriter's hub: Sir Arnel, Ma'am Diana, Sir Chits, Sir Mark, Sir Chi, Sir Rolly and a lot more.

# About the Author

Ismael Tabuñar Fortunado

I am an Engineer, an author, an inventor, a poet, a lyricist and a researcher. I am from Caloocan City, Philippines. I am an author of 16 books and three book chapters. I have four inventions. I am the author of 33 researches. I wrote over 500 poems. I am currently working on different areas of science, arts and theology. I was employed by WNS World Choice Travel as Operations Associate, UCONNECTS as Sales Agent, Bestank Manufacturing Corporation as Customer Care Agent, Maynilad Water Services, Inc. as Project employee, St. Joseph College of Novaliches, Inc. as teacher and Philippine Long Distance Telephone as Assistant Project Engineer. I joined few notable societies: National Research Council of the Philippines, Filipino Inventors Society and Philippine National Philosophical Research Society.

**He invented one of the best perpetual calendar.**
**He solved the collatz conjecture. Only the tail has a cycle. Division is repeated subtraction. The (an) IDs or identifications are (could be) infinite.**
**He solved the fermat's last theorem using difference analysis or gap analysis.**
**He solved the beal conjecture using difference analysis or gap analysis.**
**He wrote Human Kingdom, separating man from animals.**
**And a lot more.**

**Angel**

I don't want you to see
All my pains and tears.
I have to learn a proper mind.
All I see is you.

I will be lying just to see a beautiful you.
All I can recall is our music.
A beautiful angel is you.

You flew all around.
Creating wonders that's great.
My sad memories are gone.
You took them away.

Please stay with my angel.
Please bear with me.
I must have taken another look.
You took my mind away.

I still recall you hold my hands.
Praying to the almighty.
I still recall you calling me dearly.

Angel be with me, stay with me.
All I wish is about you.
The sweetness of your voice
Is too great to be heard.

**Beside you**

The seat is vacant.
My heart is too.
Sit beside me.
Don't go afar.

You introduce yourself
In a class of thirty.
You smiled so great.
No one is to blame.

Thunder is there.
And no more to sigh.
Beside you will be great.
Kindly listen to my heart.

Beside you would be nice.
Capturing my heart though.
Letting it speak.
Letting it grow fond of you.

Don't be scared.
I am the one scared.
Hope not be the creep.
You are in my sleep.

You brighten up my days.
Sitting beside you.
Cornering my thoughts.
Hope I can tell you what I feel.

Beside you is so sweet.
Like the pillow in my dream.
Like the sunshine of my days.
Like a rainbow after the rain.

**Black Heart**

Remind me on the draw.
All I think is moonlight.
Suited with suits.
Thinking of the nuts.

Black kings, black dreams.
We would seek a win.
The window broke
Down the stream.

Sunshine passed through
This lovely pairs.
What do you think?
Stay with it.

Black heart, read pairs.
Look at those crazy hands.
Would you rather lose
To let others make a win?

Are we close to this?
A gamble or a try?
What's the price after all our time?
Nothing to lose; nothing to win.

Take my time to read
A people's face, a people's mind.
Freeze each time, I see goodbye.
Sometimes we don't shine.

**Catch me**

Our dog has grown.
I gave you the best.
Say hello
To the beautiful one.

Catch me! I have fallen.
On my knees begging.
Cutting the crap.
Cutting the cake.

Together is what I dream.
Holding hands, holding dreams.
Catch me! I am loving.
Catch my breathe.

My love for you is sweet.
Sweet as the sugar.
And this is deep.
Deep as the ocean.

Catch me! I love you.
No words could contain it.
No songs could make it.
To be with you as always.

Thank you for staying.
This love will not wait.
All that you can have.
Take it. Take it.

Catch me! Then say it.
I love you and
I mean it.
For you I'm falling.

**Close your eyes, darling**

Open up your heart
Like open doors with open mind.
Throwing the dart
Not catching the dark.

Close your eyes
Close those gaps.
Like open windows.
Like open hands.

Like the snow it fleets.
Like the mountain that sings.
Like the memory of a scene.
Close your eyes, darling.

How do you see
The other side of me?
I want to give you a good memory.
I want to share you good times.

Have not seen another you.
Have not seen another blue.
Close your eyes, darling.
Meet those surprises.

To see you smile is a wonder.
To see you smile matters.
To see you grow and laugh
Close your eyes, darling.

## Cloud

Restless day it is.
No work, no pay.
Just heavy and resting.
Don't want to do anything.
Could have seen the lilies.

Today is so important.
That I almost forgot to breathe.
No melodies, no riffs.
Let me put to sleep.

Cloud my vision.
Cloud my sleep.
Covering the skies.
Covering my whys.

Fight this feeling for a while.
Laziness is at hand.
Could ask for more.
Would want to.

Hoping for bright day.
Tomorrow maybe or maybe a little while.
Missing you this day.
Missing these good lines.

Cloud, why are you here?
Don't want to sleep.
Don't want to sigh.
Life would be filled with clouds.

## Clown

Who can make you happy?
Is it a joker of me?
Funny is it I crack one.
Crack heads that's it.
The world is wide.
Wide for the people to see.

Who can make you sad?
A clown may be.
Seeing him(her) leave, an end that's it.
Who can make you cry?
Not a mime I guess.
Nodding to yes, not less.

Clown is there to be.
More than a memory.
See the shackles in his hand.
Magician on the side.

Who can make you dream?
Who can make you frown?
Clouding your thoughts.
Clowning your foughts.
Who can make you sick?
Treasure is to give.

Smile, life is short.
Having a toy is great.
May it be small.
May it be big.
Clown, I'm just here.
Here to make you happy.

**Clueless**

Don't take my hand.
Please don't take.
We plant each day.
The fortune tress.

Do I pull the petals?
Making it last.
Tomorrow will be the same.
Still seeing the shine in your eyes.

Bright lights.
You are clueless.
How you brighten my day.
Clueless, that will be.

Still weak, more than weeks.
I cannot have made luck.
Why do we seek?
A crib is good too.

There is nothing new.
I hope that goes well.
Still having you.
That won't be too sweet.

Clueless, no more clue.
I have pasted it in glue.

Bright lights.
You are clueless.
How you brighten my day.
Clueless, that will be.

**Color**

You left me blind
with a soft punch in the heart.
An odd duck with a tail.
Funny is with your name.

Red is your nose
Like the deer, Santa bear.
It is as sweet as the rose.
Not your cheeks, not your lips.

Oh how colorful it is
To hold your hand.
It brings a brighter world
Just to be with you.

Funny is it not being alone.
I still have your pen.
Mighty words will never die.
There is always a victory cry.

Look there is a rainbow.
Do you have to pull the bow?
Breaking the vase.
Trying an ace.

Attention is there to be knocking.
Holding the rose without the torn.
Listening for the birds.
Whispering your tone.

What is your true color?
What is your true blue?
I have no fine clue.
I have to say true.

**Crazy you, crazy me**

Why o why, the sun shines so bright?
Call me crazy but this is true.
Loving a friend like you.
Crazier is this line for me.

Call me crazy, crazy in love.
Love is for fools thus creating tools.
I love you. Do I need to prove it?
Stupid is what I make like this.

Comment or commend on me on what to do?
You stole my heart in front of me.
Careful with those hands, they might.
Might undo the pain of this lonely world.

Crazy you, crazy me. Crazy not.
Is there someone hurting you not?
Someone is hurting me and it is you.
You left me in the freezing rain.

Dip your fingers in the water.
You have done everything good.
Crashing tales of the heroes.
Crazy you, crazy me, crazy lines.

Shouting your name in the pouring rain.
Writing it in a beach far away.
I took this time to thank you.
I will miss those energetic flame.

I need to carry on to this life.
I will miss the times beside you.
Crazy you, crazy me, crazy beast.
Crying till this time is true.

**Day by Day**

Seeing by the benches so blue.
All I can think of is a new.
Waiting for your lover so great.
Waiting for your dreamer to pray.

Seeing you in the library, drew.
Sweet are the books like treats.
Echoing the past so true.
Wondering why the seat is untrue.

Seeing you in the bus stop for a while.
Entering the populated crowd.
Where are you heading?
Where will you might be?

Talking to myself,
Day by day, what will I do?
Against the time for a try.
Day by day, will you go?

Go off in the clouds of shade.
Wait it will rain inside.
Day by day, will it slow?
Your hair it lingers, so long.

Day by day, it kills me.
I could not say hello.
I don't have the chance.
How will I have to let go?

Day by day, I have to stop.
Take a glance, your smile so great.
It takes me to different world.
Day by day, day by day…

**Disease**

Can you please put me to sleep?
You step on me for a while.
I cannot feel my feet.
I cannot feel my heart.
Do I need to show you?

Somebody has no shoes.
Until I've seen no feet.
Disease, this is dreaded one.
Could not take this more.

Even the great crawls
Even the king obeys.
When rain touches your hand.
While this disease still creeps.

If I could not take another one.
Another madness reaches you.
While this disease creeps.
Taking all of me.
How to get away?

Each step leads me to you.
Will you be carried?
Will you mind this disease?
The heck with this.
Couldn't make a better wish.

Disease, I want to be cured.
With you I know.
I know I'll be out of disease.
In no time, no disease.

**Glimpse**

Glimpse, all you have to do is glimpse.
All you have is me.
Take a glance, you will not regret.
All I have is yours.

You took my heart and hide it.
To the woods I guess.
Hear its beat it's only you.
Make happiness its friend.

Swaying like the trees
Is my love for you honey.
Call it crazy, call it not.
Glimpse and smile is what I like.

I dedicated my life you.
Knowing that one time you will glance.
Listening to the birds chirp.
All you have to do is glimpse.

Leap you heart out hearing this.
I may not have shown the greatness of this.
Try to understand.
I am a fool, fool for you.

Glimpse, you thought of it?
So that I may see your beautiful smile.
Carry it with me as I go.
Thank God you glimpse.

**Goodbye**

Hello, you come to me like a breeze.
How sweet of you, how sweet of this.
Recalling your voice back then.
Retrace those steps.

1, 2, 3, I come close to you.
Recognize these moves.
Make you fall, make you fall.
Fall asleep I guess.

Goodbye is I have to say.
Transferring school.
Transferring cool.
I have to go.

Going to a place where no shadows meet.
Going to a place where palaces there.
Due to the time unknown.
Due to a time unforeseen.

Please stay in my heart.
But all I have is goodbye.
A proper one would do.
All I can say is none.

My thoughts are swimming.
Always at the brink.
Brink of the horizon.
Can't say more than enough.

## Hearing

Have I lost touch,
Touch of reality, its false?
Remembering the time lost.
I need to hear your voice.

Carried in the wind
Is your smile so sweet.
I carry it all around
Like a child longing.

Wondering how the good meets me?
Your name is so good.
Hearing it lightens the day.
Hearing it lightens my mood.

When can I hear those sweet words?
I have told you that you are great.
Please teach me to live.
To live with you.

When can I hear those kind words?
Comforting me till the end.
Hoping to cross the bridge
With those fine words.

Your words will let me heal.
Hearing the voice of an angel.
Hearing your voice so sweet.
Even a fool like me could speak.

I catch a cold that I could die.
May I hear those last words?
Hearing them for the last time.
Will be a memory to me.

## Heartbeat

Crippled by the past,
Hearing all the pain.
Got a strange look.
Like all is mistake.

How do we call each other?
In a heartbeat I guess.
You hear me open up.
Just like a door.

In a heartbeat you change.
And change my life.
Taking all you want.
Talking all day.

Heartbeat, in a heartbeat.
I can feel my heart.
I can't feel its beat.
Too much ice cream.

So happy that we've met,
Like you were the last one.
Ticking of the clock,
I hope you see.

In a heartbeat you change my life.
It is ok, it is great.
I just weave this.
The petals fall.

Don't mess up my heart.
Could we feel them all?
In a heartbeat,
The heartbeat knows them all.

**How is your day?**

How is your day?
Is it perfect that shine?
How is your fam-ily?
Is it good? Is it well?

Do rivers lie? Do oceans dream?
Seeing light in them.
Working till the segment lend.
Wondering the sweetness take.

How is your pet?
Does it chew, chew bones?
How is your piano?
How does it sing?

Sing with me. Dance with me.
Enjoy a time. Even for awhile.
Busy time it is.
Have you seen a stressed beam?

How is your day?
How is your week?
Making the memories unblink.
How is your dream?
How is your friend?

I'd rather lie.
No reasons why.
I'd rather live.
All reasons try.

How is your day?
How is your May?
Knitting these lines.

Doing for you.
How is your find?

How is your day?
How is your day?
Molding a clay.
Having your day.
Singing, "How is your day?"

**I am a shadow.**

Call it crazy, call it weak.
You have seen it all.
My weakness and all.
You were there all through out.

Forget me not, I'm here to stay.
I'm your shadow, a part of you.
You care too well.
You smile too good.

Let the sun shine your face.
Even the corner of your face.
Each good you grew.
Each tear you shed.
I'm at your back.

So let this darkness speak.
I'm with you.
How can I not be there?
The sun shines with you.

Call it crazy, somehow fun
To be with you all along.
You have seen through me.
I am a shadow.

Let the sun shine to you.
Even the smile of your face.
Each wall you climb.
Each fears you fought.
I am a shadow to your thoughts.

**I love it when it rains.**

I love it when it rains.
My tears can't be seen.
My hurts can't be cast.
My socks get wet still.

I love it when it rains.
My calls can't be match.
My screams don't touch the ground.
My whisper sounds deadly.

I love it when it rains.
I am a nobody that it aches.
I am nobody to fall for.
I am singing my last.

I love it when it rains.
Music of the rain is so great.
Like laser cutting the twig.
Like honesty too deep.

I love it when it rains.
Silly me that I give
The long stem is green.
The flowers cry too.

I love it when it rains.
I should not fall for one.
Is there someone waiting for me?
The drop of rain in my palm.

I love it when it rains.
I love it when it rains.
I love it when it rains.
No one could see my pains.

**I never had you.**

Standing for a while,
Waiting for the bus.
The rain just poured.
You don't have a coat.

I have the umbrella
To shield you on the rain.
It's just another bad day
Until that you came.

I never had you.
You look too far.
Reminiscing all those times.
Regretting all those lines.

You didn't say a word.
Neglecting all those fears.
You were loved and cared.
I don't take the steps.

Close to you I guess.
All that is what I want.
Never knew you all along.
Saying the proper goodbye.

Remedy this heart.
I hope I can make it.
Just stay with me for a while.
I never had you.

Saying all these lines.
I wish I have the courage to say.
Some things were not meant.
Meeting someone like you.

**Inconceivable**

We part ways
Is it because of me
Do I wonder, you're
Inconceivable

You took the left turn
I took the right one.
I can't believe that
You're inconceivable

I did something wrong
You can't forgive me though
I hope you are alright but
You're inconceivable

This life could be
Very inconceivable
Gonna think of it
Very inconceivable

Life is good
Life is a present
Sometimes you can't move
Life is sometimes gonna be
Inconceivable

Take the time
Something you like
Something you remember
Very inconceivable

**Just walk away**

I give myself to you.
Wholehearted and that scares me.
I know that you won't love me.
Care to be with me?

It took me wine to say this.
All the heart I missed.
If you could just walk away.
I don't want you to see.

Just walk away.
I don't want you to see.
See these flaws and tears.
I'll just accept what you give.

Think of me as a friend.
Who just say things I regret.
I never could have thought.
You belong to someone else.

Just walk away.
This pain would go away.
All the dreams I had for us.
Seems everything is distant now.

Take all of me
Don't just walk away.
Leave me hanging.
Will I be just alone?

Just walk away.
Leave me breathless.
I will take it.
Just walk away.

**Kiss**

I see you, my lover.
You caught my hand waving.
I laugh with my mistakes.
Knowing you are a joker.

Funny with all the punch.
Can I still see you dance?
Weak are the knees,
Wanting to pray aside.

Kiss, so lovely sight.
Kiss all pretty might.
Kiss, sharing the breathe.
Kiss, the passionate melt.
Kiss, the face aglows.
Kiss, so heaven knows.

Just for a while
I have to think.
Do I have you?
I don't want to blink.

Leave me with kisses.
Leave be with bes.
Running to you quick.
Happy is this time.

All is there.
Any would be lame.
How to make you happy?
With a kiss maybe.

Kiss, completely free.
The whole me I give.

Please accept for I fall.
Each time, each night, each fall.

**Lie**

You are beautiful, you will see.
Trying to get attention especially you.
Making something out of the blue.
Dealing with this disease.
Making something out of the dream.
Out of my head, I said.

I'm telling the truth, yet you
You feel it s a lie.
My parents told me to not make one.
If only you could stay.

I won't make a lie.
Catching all the stars.
Giving you the moon.
Moving all clouds.
All I have is words.

You are beautiful, you will see.
Trying to get attention especially you.
Making something out of the blue.
Waking out of this dream.
Out of my head, I cry.

Time is afloat. Time is near.
Woke up to a bright light.
Have seen the train pass.
Have drank a cold water.
Have not hold your hand.

Still writing this lie.
Out of my head, I lie.

**Love**

Take all of me,
I am yours truly.
Walking down the aisle
Is your dream.

Seeing all your friends.
Happiness that you seek.
To have a family,
To have a home.

Love is all you want.
Not tragedies, not pain.
Wake up beside you.
Woke up to greet you.

When will this valentines end?
Another cold December so it seems.
Grasping all the air.
Feeling all insane.

At ease with this pain,
All we want is this love.
Love endures,
Endures all things.

Crying all you want for love.
I never had the feeling.
The feeling of being alone.
Love captures me.

**Loving Myself**

I'm half crazy.
Crazy in love with you.
Will my words matter?
Your smile matters.

I commit myself to God.
But to meet you is good too.
You pick me up.
Cathastrophic me.
What have I just said?

Star gazing, much star there is.
All I have is this pen.
Have not wondered when.
You have a good pet.

Losing myself, losing myself.
All I ponder is you.
Like I loose mind.
To someone, not a stranger.

Will you take an incomplete?
Losing myself, I die each day.
Have never felt this before.
Don't stop me from falling.

I see your smile.
I see your tears.
You smile so cute.
You fear the doors closing in.

**Nights**

Summer nights
Will the start of winter?
These cold nights,
Will you still remember?

Winter nights
Will they end in November?
These colorful lights,
Will you see me sober?

De javu, kidding this lines
All I think is you.
The nights are longer.
The days are fine.

Sober nights
Will I still remember?
These fun times,
Will they end in December?

Just remember those laughs we had.
I see that glow that you have.
Listen to me carefully.
Killing this time.

Does the night seem fair?
Longer do we stay.
Say those words when asleep.
Nights oh those nights.

## Pen

All I have is this.
Can't sing or dance.
Even run or fly.
But still can I have your glance?

Dreaming of you all day long.
Knowing that would go.
Knowing you won't fall.
All I have is this soul.

What matters now
Is that you look my way.
Even for a moment.
Even for a while.

Can I have you for a while?
I don't have the looks.
I don't even have the skills.
Even for a while, can I see your smile?

This pen is my pillow.
This pen is my wall.
This pen is my sun.
I would not ask for more.

To call you mine.
To be with you in time.
Will I reach you
In this writing of mine?

**Rain**

When you close your eyes
And the rain falls down,
The tears unrecognized.

You hold back your feelings.
Letting the shadows,
Beat the most of you.

Thanks to the rain
You cannot see the shadow.
Time is fast leaving.

It wakes you up,
Back to your senses.
Creating more ripples.

It is cold, you need something
More than umbrella,
More than sweater, just hugs.

Thanks to the rain
We sat a while and drink tea.
Its freezing here, hear my heart.

Thanks to the rain
I met you, you are beautiful.
You were crying.

## Rainfall

Sitting on the branches,
We laugh with ease.
Seeing all the building,
We had it all.

You were on my mind
You were on my sleep.
I still recall all the overhaul.
Even the crowd, even the fall.

Rainfall, I touched them fall.
Watery day, seeing all the rain.
Scared of the flood.
Not of the boat.

You were on my mind.
Caught up in the streets.
Listening the falling rain.
Singing all day long.

When will this end?
Just like the rainfall.
It slips your fingertips.
Will I make it in time?

Rain fall, rain slips.
Seeing this rainfall.
Will this be my last?
Writing all the way.

Rainfall until this is undone.
I still recall writing this.
Seeing the rainfall,
Catching a glimpse.

**Risky**

Given a chance,
Will you take me?
Plucking the petal,
Will you see me?

You are with a good man.
I am with a no one.
All I see is your beauty.
All I know is I thirst.

All I can do is wait.
Sing you this song and wait.
Risky is this this tone that I die.
Seeing you is a lie.

Singing you this song that I wait.
I am very sorry that I am late.
Should I give my heart to someone else?
Should I dream of a heartache?

Scared to make the first line.
Scared to try the lost time.
Will I just press escape?
Or be with you in time?

I hate this risk.
Will I take it? Foolish me.
Call your name to mine.
I'd rather wait for this.

This is me, just writing a song.
A wrong melody but we.
A risk it is, a risk it must.
This will past till three.

**She got you**

Oh my friend, she got you.
Over and under, she found you.
Taking your weapon.
Taking your treasure.

You are left unguarded.
You are left naked.
Stripped to pieces.
Broken like the glass.
Wondering the blast.

Oh my friend, she had you.
With a joke or with a smile.
Your alter ego shrinks into two.
Another you, another flew.

You are left adjacent.
You are left to dwell.
Stripped to rawness.
Broken like the pearls.
Wondering at last.

She got you, on your knees.
Begging, oh begging please.
Why is it that you clash.
Silenced by that wish.

You are left awkward.
When will you tell her?
How you feel about her.
Have courage my friend.

**She**

She will take your boredom.
She will take your cat.
Go to a place where no one's at.
Humming to the tune of some.

Will you gave her a drink?
Will that make you both sick?
Everytime I think of her, I sigh.
Why won't you make her believe?

She wears a brace that of queens.
She talks like a queen.
She gathers like a prank.
You will lose like a river out of water.

I'm gonna confess my hurts to her.
Like the winding of the clock.
Like the falling of the leaves.
This is her story, her love.

She tells, " Your life is good."
Don't chase those girls' goodbyes.
She yells, "Mind those ties."
Don't fret a goodbye.

Carry those straw not haste.
Lines full of sorrow, full of blame.
Were you made of this?
A beautiful face and beautiful heart.

No one can deny your love.
The love that heals any wounds.
Warm words that means a lot.
Perhaps I could see you still.

## Sleep

Can't close my, have to see you.
Wrote you a note but it has to go.
I can't see you well, have to wait.
No more rhyme, no more gloss.
Still can't sleep, I wonder why.

Can't wish because you don't want to.
Still carry a baggage.
A baggage of telling you.
Can't eat until this is through.

Can't move, I want to move.
Waiting in line, the touch of pen.
Shadows of despair.
I want to sleep.

They say pray for you.
All I guess its false.
False to be loving you.

Can't sleep and it hurts.
Crying with a shoulder.
And will this make me sleep?
Can't find the words maybe goodbye.

Wherever you go, please take care.
I can't find another you.
Only planets, only plants.
We don't have something in common.
Still dreaming of you.
Afar you go.

**Storm**

Set in a storm,
Is our love story.
It aches to feel this.
Empty smile, empty hands.

We are a mess.
Nowhere to be found.
Perfect tragedy, perfect storm.
Nowhere to plant the seeds.

Gazing only in your eyes.
I feel love all along.
But this is a sad song.
I could only think this is wrong.

Be in a hurry,
Time is at war.
Not hearing the birds
On finding their nests.

Dive in my mind.
We will make it through.
Through the time that misaligned.
Without a piece of a whole.

Storm so cold, against the wall.
Where I can't scream.
Severe is this pain.
But you were there.

Only fate can heal.
The storm has passed.
For this is a sad song.
We would endure.

**Trees Cry**

Trees aglow, trees afloat.
Afloat in my wishing dream.
Baby, can I call you mine?
Call me yours truly.

Trees cry seeing us break.
Break in seasons' sweat.
Seeing you this time is a sin.
You are with a good man, I see.

Tell the kids of love so great.
The eye of the plant is with the leaves.
On its tip I guess.
When it leaves, the grasp falls.

Keep it clean and true.
Loving the nature and you.
Nothing is waste; nothing to wait.
Trees try, trees bye.

Trees cry, would you not see?
Beyond the time, beyond the line.
Under and over, over and over.
Confusing the emotion, beat.

Fly high over the trees.
Root under fields, create fruits.
Weed out those feeling alone.
Reach for the sun anew.

Trees cry, they cry.
Sad and happy, they seem.
Trees cry, why lie?
Sad and happy they dream.

**You Are Unkind**

You got fangs that pierce.
Out of this world and I bleed.
You got claws, pointed ones that kills.
You walk with class, too much.

You take me to the underworld.
It was too dark and too shallow.
I thought it was hot.
It was cold, there too cold.
You came that is unkind.

You took my smile.
So please give it back.
My only smile.
You are unkind.
Not my kind.

Truth be said like an open sea.
You crossed borders.
Are you seeking home?
Will you take mine?

Tell me how's it there?
Where you grew up.
You are unkind.
Not of this world.

Can I call you mine?
You can be kind.
Singing all this line.
Knowing this crime.
You are unkind.

**Unsaid Lines**

You were correct all along.
I should have thought that.
Crispy NO, why is that?
I should have said more.
Worrying of error, I blame myself.

You were great all along.
People love you and drowning.
Turn around, people follow.
The dire might of you.

Candy for me for I lost.
Lost this dignity, lost this place.
A home I see.
Turn around and people choose.
Choose to be you.

Unsaid lines, I have good intentions.
It was not enough lasting a while.
Cannot have the chance to make you smile.
I have untied the knot.
The knot of fullness.

Like a levite of wars.
The sword befalls me.
How could I said better.
Unsaid lines are left of me.

It is late to have said.
These lines still the same.
Have not tied a knot.
Unsaid lines are left of me.

**Weird**

Is taking time worthwhile?
To write something more than blue.
Could I really take something.
Will it matter? Does it glow?

No rhyme, no family, no care.
All I have is music.
All I have is sound.
But do I have a voice?

Weird is this love for you.
As a fan, the wind blows.
I'm sinking, drowning, unbreathing.
Weird, weird, weird, weird.

What it feels, it feels cold.
Call it music, call it nuisance.
Have to make you one.

Because its weird, because unsieved.
What does it mean to laugh?
Cloud with rainbows.
Rice with salt.

Sometime to fall, fall harder and fast.
What you say is true.
Net seems so dry.
Do I need to always fry.

Something to be proud of.
You may no want to see me.
Sometimes its weird.
Weird to see a call.

**You are my baby**

Sing with me oh baby
Dance with me with care
Catching you the stars
Telling you all stories
Wondering this time
You are my baby

I am lost in you glance
I'm your slave
Baby you are great
Don't want to lose sight of you

I will tell you sweet secrets
I will tell you sweet dreams
For us to live a good memory
Catch you when you fall
Fall in my arms

Treasure some, bury sum
Walk with me to the sun
Baby, don't you cry
Hush Oh hush

Sing with me
Dance with me
Catching all those tears
Telling you all dreams
Wondering with you
You are my baby

Tell you the truth
Of this world and beyond
Heaven is where must we belong
You are my baby